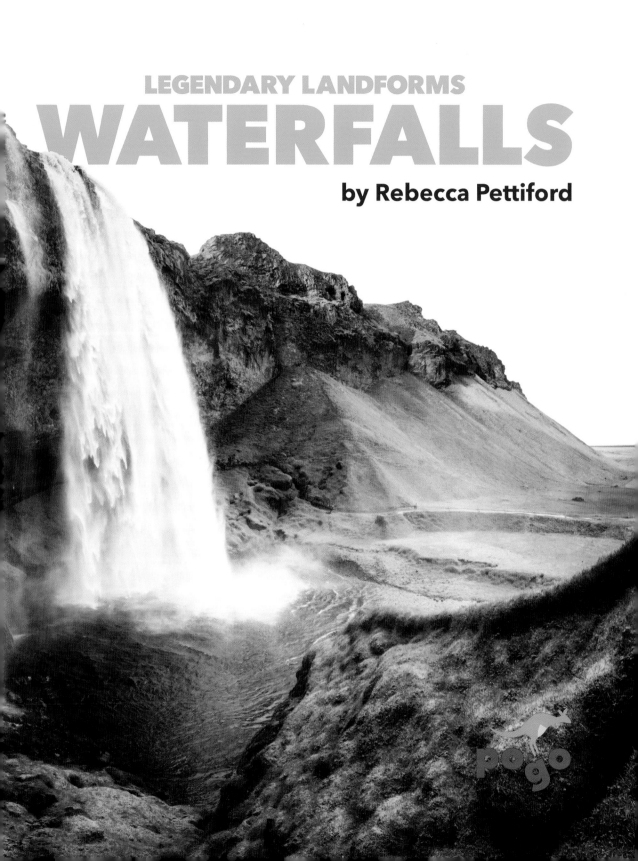

LEGENDARY LANDFORMS
WATERFALLS

by Rebecca Pettiford

POGO

Ideas for Parents and Teachers

Pogo Books let children practice reading informational text while introducing them to nonfiction features such as headings, labels, sidebars, maps, and diagrams, as well as a table of contents, glossary, and index.

Carefully leveled text with a strong photo match offers early fluent readers the support they need to succeed.

Before Reading

• "Walk" through the book and point out the various nonfiction features. Ask the student what purpose each feature serves.

• Look at the glossary together. Read and discuss the words.

Read the Book

• Have the child read the book independently.

• Invite him or her to list questions that arise from reading.

After Reading

• Discuss the child's questions. Talk about how he or she might find answers to those questions.

• Prompt the child to think more. Ask: Have you ever seen a waterfall or a picture of one? How would you describe it?

Pogo Books are published by Jump!
5357 Penn Avenue South
Minneapolis, MN 55419
www.jumplibrary.com

Library of Congress Cataloging-in-Publication Data

Names: Pettiford, Rebecca, author.
Title: Waterfalls / by Rebecca Pettiford.
Description: Minneapolis, MN: Jump!, Inc., [2018]
Series: Legendary landforms |
"Pogo Books are published by Jump!."
Includes index. | Audience: Ages 7-10.
Identifiers: LCCN 2016056362 (print)
LCCN 2017000029 (ebook)
ISBN 9781620317112 (hard cover: alk. paper)
ISBN 9781620317495 (pbk.)
ISBN 9781624965883 (e-book)
Subjects: LCSH: Waterfalls–Juvenile literature.
Niagara Falls (N.Y. and Ont.)–Juvenile literature.
Classification: LCC GB1403.8 .P48 2018 (print)
LCC GB1403.8 (ebook) | DDC 551.48/4–dc23
LC record available at https://lccn.loc.gov/2016056362

Editor: Kirsten Chang
Book Designer: Leah Sanders
Photo Researcher: Leah Sanders

Photo Credits: Andrew Sproule/Getty, cover; Standret/Shutterstock, 1; ZM_Photo/Shutterstock, 3; Stuart Westmorland/SuperStock, 4; agustavop/iStock, 5; ThanyathornP/Shutterstock, 6-7; Susan E. Degginger/Superstock, 8-9; Ray Bulson/Getty, 10-11; Kiattipong/Shutterstock, 12-13; Adnan Vejzovic/Shutterstock, 13; Feargus Cooney/Getty, 13; holbox/Shutterstock, 13; judytally/Shutterstock, 13; Androsov/Thinkstock, 14; Ron_Thomas/iStock, 15; CrackerClips Stock Media/Shutterstock, 16-17; Olesya Baron/Shutterstock, 18-19; Elena Elisseeva/Shutterstock, 20-21; Puripat Lertpunyaroj/Shutterstock, 23.

Printed in the United States of America at Corporate Graphics in North Mankato, Minnesota.

TABLE OF CONTENTS

CHAPTER 1

FALLING WATER

Imagine you are hiking in the mountains. You hear running water up ahead. You get closer. The sound grows to a roar. You reach a clearing. It's a waterfall!

A waterfall is a **landform**. It is the part of a river or stream that drops over a steep, rocky **ledge**. It falls into a pool of water below. A waterfall can also be a series of shorter drops along a river or stream.

Waterfalls are caused by **erosion**. As water flows, it carries **sediment** such as sand and rocks. It wears away the soft rock in river and stream beds. It leaves a hard, rocky ledge. The water falls over the ledge.

What are the parts of a waterfall?

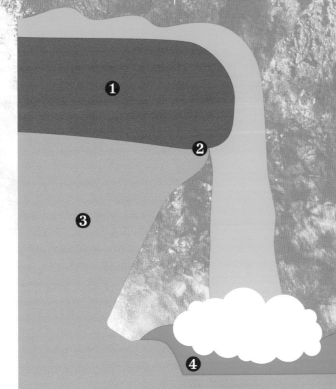

❶ hard rock
❷ overhang
❸ soft rock
❹ plunge pool

Waterfalls also cause erosion. At the bottom of the falls, the water churns quickly. It eats away at the soft rock in the riverbed. In time, the waterfall gets taller. Sometimes, pieces of the rocky ledge break off. When this happens, the falls **recede**.

glacier

Earthquakes, **volcanoes**, and **glaciers** create waterfalls, too. They cause the land to shift. This changes the height in the bed of a river or stream. With such a sudden change in height, a stream or river quickly becomes a waterfall.

There are many types of waterfalls. Their names often describe how they look. Here are four:

1) Fan waterfalls fan out wide as they descend.

2) Block waterfalls descend in a wide sheet.

3) Tiered waterfalls drop in steps.

4) Punchbowl waterfalls fall into a wide, round pool.

CHAPTER 2

THE POWER OF WATER

Falling water has a lot of power. It can be used to make **hydroelectricity**.

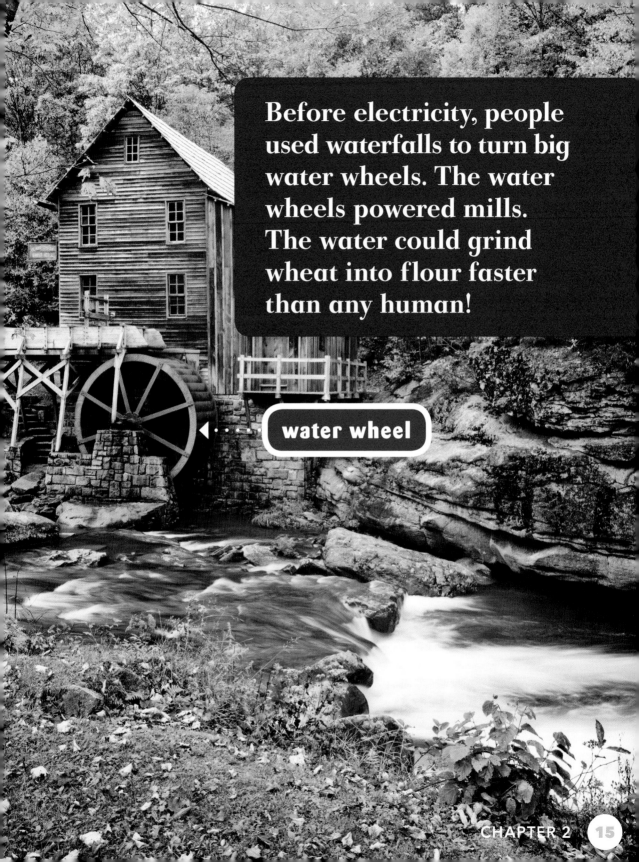

Before electricity, people used waterfalls to turn big water wheels. The water wheels powered mills. The water could grind wheat into flour faster than any human!

water wheel

generator · · · · · ▶

When a natural waterfall is not available, humans can create their own. People build **dams**. This directs a strong flow of water to **turbines**. Turbines power generators. Generators give us electricity.

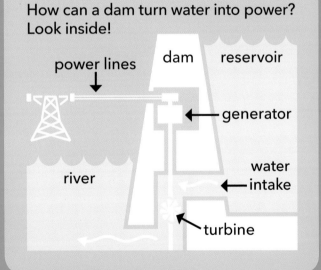

TAKE A LOOK!

How can a dam turn water into power? Look inside!

power lines

dam

reservoir

generator

river

water intake

turbine

CHAPTER 3

NIAGARA FALLS

Niagara Falls is a famous waterfall in North America. It is made up of three different falls. It is so big that it is in two countries! The falls act as a natural border between the two countries.

United States

These falls formed more than 10,000 years ago. Melting ice from a glacier caused Lake Erie to flood. The Niagara River formed. It cut through the land. Over time, it formed a **gorge**. This became Niagara Falls.

Canada

Scientists believe these falls may be gone in about 50,000 years. Why? Erosion never stops. Today, Niagara Falls recedes about 12 inches (30 centimeters) every year. But don't worry. You still have time to visit this legendary landform!

ACTIVITIES & TOOLS

TRY THIS!

MAKE A WATERFALL

Make a small waterfall with items you find in your home and in nature.

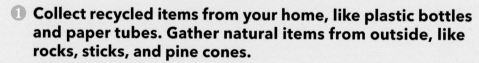

What You Need:
- paper and pencil
- water
- scissors
- rubber cement
- recycled and natural materials
- large plastic container to hold the water

1. Collect recycled items from your home, like plastic bottles and paper tubes. Gather natural items from outside, like rocks, sticks, and pine cones.

2. Think about how your waterfall will look. Draw a picture of it.

3. Build your waterfall in the large plastic container. Build a strong base. Try putting rocks in a pile for this.

4. Look at your materials. Pine cones, tubes, straws, and plastic bottles cut in half the long way are things you could use to build. Think of things that will let the water fall in unusual ways. Use the rubber cement only if you need it to glue things together. Too much cement can make the waterfall messy.

5. Pour water over the top of your waterfall. See how the water flows. Make changes to the structure if you want to change the flow of water.

GLOSSARY

dams: Walls built across a river or stream to stop it from flowing.

earthquakes: Sudden shakings of part of Earth's surface.

erosion: The slow destruction of something by water, wind, and ice.

glaciers: Large bodies of ice that move slowly on the land's surface and shape it as they move.

gorge: A deep, narrow area between hills or mountains.

hydroelectricity: Electricity produced from machines that are powered by moving water.

landform: A natural feature of Earth's surface.

ledge: A flat rock surface that sticks out.

recede: To move away slowly.

sediment: Material such as stones and sand deposited by water and wind.

turbines: Machines that capture energy from a moving liquid through use of a wheel that moves in response to water pressure.

volcanoes: Vents in the earth that sometimes send out rocks, ash, and lava in a sudden explosion.

INDEX

TO LEARN MORE

Learning more is as easy as 1, 2, 3.

1) Go to www.factsurfer.com

2) Enter "legendarywaterfalls" into the search box.

3) Click the "Surf" button to see a list of websites.

With factsurfer, finding more information is just a click away.